God's Baby Animals

Written by Marjorie Re████ ██ Courtney Rice
Illustrated by Kathryn Marlin

ISBN 978-1-4964-0130-4

Printed in China

20	19	18	17		
7	6	5	4	3	2

Tyndale House Publishers, Inc.
Carol Stream, Illinois

God made animals!

"So God made the wild animals, the tame animals and all the small crawling animals to produce more of their own kind. God saw that this was good." *Genesis 1:25*

A baby raccoon is a kit.

Find food, kit!

A baby koala is a joey.

Stay safe, joey!

A baby dog is a pup.

Have fun, pup!

A baby giraffe is a calf.

Reach high, calf!

A baby horse is a foal.

Don't fall, foal!

A baby tiger is a cub.

Keep warm, cub!

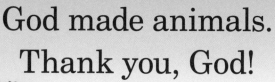

God made animals.
Thank you, God!

Let's Talk about It

1. Who made the animals?

2. What is a baby raccoon called?

3. What is a baby koala called?

4. What is a baby horse called?

5. What is your favorite baby animal?

Matching Items

cub

kit

calf

foal

Word Search

```
Q  Y  K  I  T  V
B  F  E  S  F  W
X  F  O  O  C  T
X  L  Y  A  J  F
M  A  J  N  L  M
R  C  A  R  A  E
```

Find these words

CALF • FOAL • JOEY • KIT

Craft Activity

Make a baby animal collage!

Things you will need:
- old magazines
- crayons/markers/stickers/other decorative items
- scissors
- glue
- paper

What to do:

1. Look though old magazines to find pictures of baby animals.

2. Cut out the pictures that you like.

3. Glue the pictures onto your paper.

4. Ask your mom or dad to help you learn the names of the baby animals and write them next to the pictures.

5. Decorate the paper with stickers, crayons, or any other items you want.

6. Hang your collage on the wall or on the refrigerator so you can see your favorite babies whenever you want!

COLORING PAGE

COLORING PAGE

Shape a lifestyle of faith expression in your child

— Our passion is to provide a creative outlet for kids to express their faith in a fun and meaningful way. Cultivate a deeper connection as you teach your child about the impact of God's love, building a legacy of relationship, creativity, and faith to last a lifetime.

Using interactive games, puzzles, and other activities, **Faith That Sticks resources** are a great go-to place for parents who want to teach their kids to love God and to know how much he loves them!

More about Reading Levels

PRE-READERS

Books appropriate for pre-readers have

- pictures that reinforce the text
- simple words
- short, simple sentences
- repetition of words and patterns
- large print

BEGINNING READERS

Books appropriate for beginning readers have

- pictures that reinforce the text
- intermediate words
- longer sentences
- simple stories
- dialogue between story characters

INDEPENDENT READERS

Books appropriate for independent readers have

- less need for pictorial support with the text
- more advanced vocabulary
- paragraphs
- longer stories
- more complex subjects

"There are perhaps no days of our childhood we lived so fully as those we spent with a favorite book." — MARCEL PROUST